# A WILLIAM MATHIAS ORGA[N]

*To Christopher Morris*
*musician, publisher, friend*

## RECESSIONAL

WILLIAM MATHIAS
(Opus 96, No. 4)

**Allegro moderato, sempre vivace** ( ♩ = *c.*112)

Printed in Great Britain

OXFORD UNIVERSITY PRESS, MUSIC DEPARTMENT, GREAT CLARENDON STREET, OXFORD OX2 6DP

6

# PROCESSIONAL

WILLIAM MATHIAS
(1964)

*To Michael Smythe*

# JUBILATE

I   Great
II  Swell
III Solo or Choir

WILLIAM MATHIAS
(Opus 67, No.2)

**Molto vivace e ritmico** ( ♪ = ♪ throughout)

15

# POSTLUDE

WILLIAM MATHIAS
(1962)

# CANZONETTA

WILLIAM MATHIAS
(Opus 78, No. 2)

# CHORALE

WILLIAM MATHIAS
(Easter 1966)

*To Sir David Willcocks on the occasion of his Inauguration of the
new organ at The Royal College of Organists, 7th October 1967.*

# TOCCATA GIOCOSA

WILLIAM MATHIAS
(Opus 36, No. 2)